WHEN Does the internet face traffic?

Om KIDZ
An imprint of Om Books International

AF516730

Contents

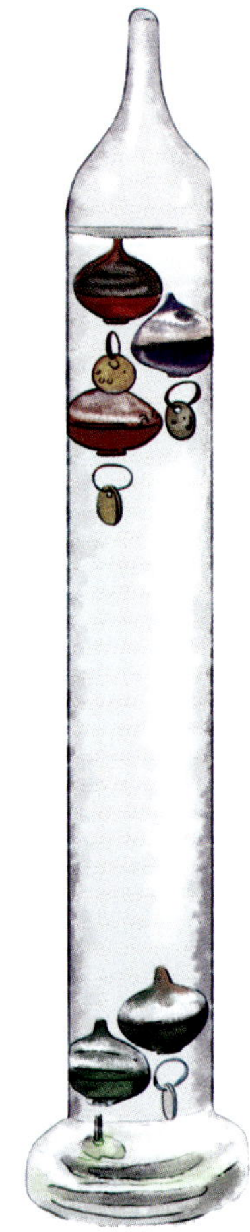

- When did humans start making stone tools? 3
- When was iron first used for making tools? 3
- When were bricks invented? 4
- When did humans begin growing crops? 4
- When was the alphabet invented? 5
- When was the pencil invented? 5
- When was the first ball pen invented? 6
- When was the digital pen invented? 6
- When did Romans invent the first basic concrete? 7
- When was cement invented? 7
- When were the first eyeglasses invented? 8
- When were contact lenses invented? 8
- When was the first parachute invented? 9
- When was hot air balloon invented? 9
- When was the mercury thermometer invented? 10
- When was the barometer invented? 10
- When were microphones invented? 11
- When was the first speech synthesizer invented? 11
- When was sound first recorded and played back on metal foil? 12
- When was the digital audio player invented? 12
- When was the first electric washing machine invented? 13
- When was the dishwasher invented? 13
- When was the first Smartphone invented? 14
- When was the first automated reader invented? 14
- When was the supercomputer invented? 15
- When does the internet face traffic? 15
- Index 16

When did humans start making stone tools?

Almost 3 million years ago! Stone tools were first made by early humans in East Africa. Early men called *Homo habilis* were the first group of modern humans to make tools. They made different kinds of stone tools like fist-sized hunks of rock and sharp flakes. These tools were known as the Oldowan and used to hunt animals.

Pocket fact

Stone Age!
The time in history when early humans used tools and weapons made out of stone is referred to as Stone Age.

Find out

The Stone Age was divided into three periods. Find their names.

When was iron first used for making tools?

Iron is found in rocks called iron ore. It was discovered by early humans in around 1200 BCE. But the techniques to purify iron and put it to use were first developed in the Middle East after 1500 BCE. Iron could be melted and poured into a mould to make weapons and tools. Iron objects were made by smiths i.e. metal workers.

When were bricks invented?

Bricks were first made around 6,000 years ago. The earliest bricks were made from clay-bearing earth or mud and usually dried in the sun until they were strong enough for use. The oldest discovered bricks date back to around 7500 BC. These were found at Tell Aswad, in the upper Tigris region and in southeast Anatolia close to Diyarbakir.

Pocket fact

The bond!

The patterns created when bricks are laid on the courses are called the bond. To create a durable structure such as fences or houses, the bricks are placed by using mortar. This type of construction is called brickwork.

Find out

When were fruits first grown?

When did humans begin growing crops?

Prior to growing crops, human beings were hunters and gatherers. Farming began around 10,000 BCE. Early men, who had travelled to different places in search of food, began to harvest wild grains they found growing there. They scattered spare grains on the ground to grow more food. Over time, people began to live in settled communities and grew crops on nearby land.

When was the alphabet invented?

The history of the alphabet started in ancient Egypt in around 2700 BCE. Egyptian writing had a set of some 22 hieroglyphs to represent syllables. But the evolution of modern-day alphabet involved two important steps. The first was the invention of consonantal writing system known as North Semitic by the Phoenicians between 1700 and 1500 BCE. The second was the invention of characters for representing vowels by the Greeks. This happened between 800 and 700 BCE.

Pocket fact

The word *alphabet* comes from the first two letters of the Greek alphabet—alpha and beta.

Find out

When was the eraser invented?

When was the pencil invented?

In 1564! Pencils were invented after a large deposit of graphite was found in Borrowdale, England. This new material was brittle but was good for making marks. The graphite ore was cut into large sheets that were then cut into square chunks and fitted into hand-carved wooden holders. The modern pencil was invented by Nicolas-Jacques Conte in 1795.

When was the first ball pen invented?

The ballpoint pen was invented in 1888 by John J. Loud who was attempting to make a writing instrument that could be used for writing on rough surfaces such as wood, coarse wrapping-paper, and other articles. The pen had a small rotating steel ball, held in place by a socket. The pen could be used to mark rough surfaces such as leather but it was very rough for letter-writing.

Pocket fact

The smallest fountain pen!
The 'Nanofountain Probe' is the smallest fountain pen on record. It can write lines that are just 40 nanometre in width.

Find out

What is a stylus? How is it different from a digital pen?

When was the digital pen invented?

A digital pen is an input device which is used to capture the handwriting or brush strokes of a user. It converts handwritten analog information created using "pen and paper" into digital data. This digital data can be utilized in various applications. Digital pens were invented in the early 2000s. They are usually used in conjunction with a digital notebook.

When did Romans invent the first basic concrete?

In the late 3rd century BC! Roman concrete also called opus caementicium was made by adding volcanic dust called pozzolana to mortar made of a mixture of lime or gypsum, brick or rock pieces and water. The concrete was of excellent quality. It was used to build monuments, large buildings, roads and bridges.

Pocket fact

Let's build underwater!
Concrete is one of the only materials used for underwater structures such as dams and submerged bridge piers.

Find out

Which is the largest concrete structure in the world?

When was cement invented?

Cement was invented in 1824 by an English man Joseph Aspdin. He produced it by burning finely ground chalk and clay in a kiln until the carbon dioxide was removed. He called the cement Portland Cement. This is because the concrete made from it looked like high-quality Portland stone, a widely-used building stone in England.

Eyeglasses are believed to have been invented between 1268 and 1289 in Italy. The earliest eyeglasses were quite different from the ones today. They were just lenses held in front of the eyes or balanced on the nose. Eyeglasses with side or temple pieces that rest over the ear were advertised in 1728 and bifocals were invented by Benjamin Franklin in 1784.

Pocket fact

Reading aid!
The first vision aid was invented around 1000 AD. It was called a reading stone and was created for the far-sighted. It was a glass sphere, and resembled the magnifying glass.

Find out

What are glasses also known as?

When were contact lenses invented?

The contact lens was invented in 1887 by a Swiss physician A.E. Fick. These lenses were made of glass and were heavy. They also covered the entire eye surface, were difficult to fit and exerted an uncomfortable pressure on the eyeball. Further developments were made when plastic contact lenses were invented in 1938 and the corneal contact lens in 1950.

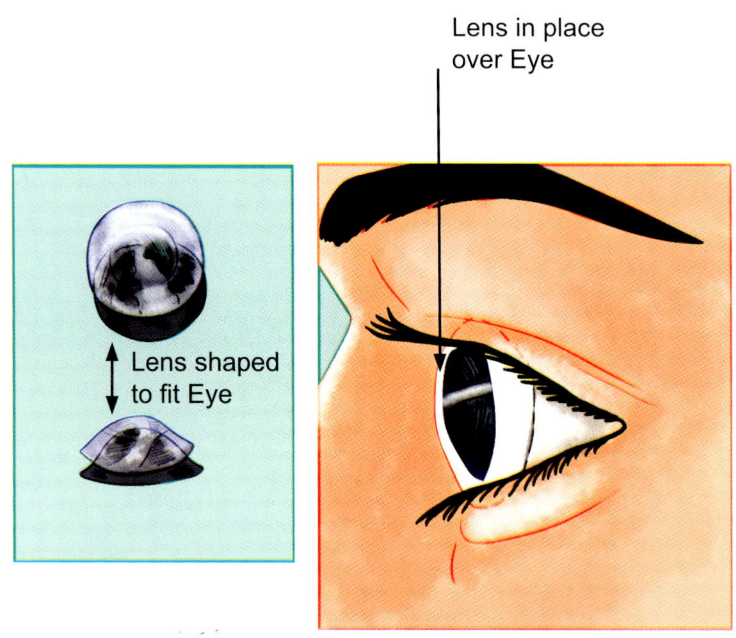

When was the first parachute invented?

Parachutes had been imagined and sketched by Abbas Ibn Firnas and Leonardo Da Vinci before its invention. In 1595, the Croatian inventor Faust Vrančić designed a parachute-like device. But the first modern parachute was invented by Sebastien Lenormand in 1783. It is believed that he mounted the tower of the Montpellier Observatory in France and jumped with a 14-foot (4.3-metre) parachute, landing unharmed.

Find out

What are present day hot air balloons made up of?

Pocket fact

Flying man!
The early parachute design was called "Homo Volans" which means Flying Man.

When was hot air balloon invented?

In the late 1700s! In 1766, Henry Cavendish proposed the idea that objects can be lifted from Earth using hydrogen. This idea was taken a step further by Joseph Michel Montgolfier from France in 1782. He used a silk bag filled with hot air and made it rise and fly for 10 minutes. Michael and his brother Jacques-Etienne worked further and in September, 1783 they made a balloon using a large spherical bag filled with hot air. This eventually led to the invention of modern hot air balloons.

When was the mercury thermometer invented?

In 1714! The mercury thermometer with a standardized scale, was invented by the German physicist Daniel Gabriel Fahrenheit. It was made of a bulb containing mercury attached to a glass tube of narrow diameter. In 1724, Daniel also introduced the standard temperature scale, the Fahrenheit Scale, that was used to record changes in temperature.

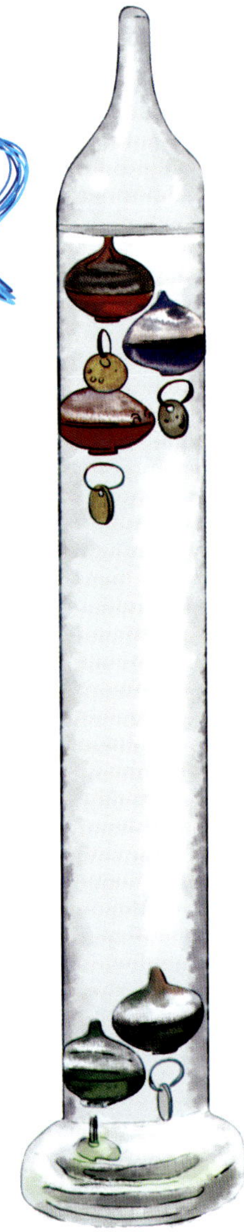

Pocket fact

I named it!
The credit for naming the barometer goes to an Englishman named Robert Boyle. He took the name from two Greek words baros and meter in 1665. The meaning of these words is measuring weight.

Find out

What are the three major temperature scales for use in the thermometer?

When was the barometer invented?

In the mid-17th century! A barometer is a device used to measure atmospheric pressure. The mercury barometer is the oldest type of barometer. It was invented by the Italian physicist Evangelista Torricelli in 1643. It was made using a 10-m long glass tube filled with water. But this was quite inconvenient so Torricelli reconstructed it using a four-foot long glass tube filled with mercury inverted into a dish of mercury. The level of mercury dropped and rose according to the atmospheric pressure.

When were microphones invented?

The first microphone was invented in 1877. It was called a carbon microphone and composed of two electrical contacts separated by a thin layer of carbon. One contact was attached to a diaphragm that vibrated when struck by a sound wave. The other was connected to the output. It was the first microphone that enabled proper voice telephony.

Find out

Which scientist was greatly helped by the speech synthesizer?

Pocket fact

Microphones were used initially for talking on the telephone as radio transmitters. As transmitters they were used to help pass on waves carrying messages or signals.

When was the first speech synthesizer invented?

In the late 1700s! The first speech synthesizer was invented by Wolfgang von Kempelen. It consisted of a pressure chamber for the lungs, a vibrating reed that acted as vocal cords, and a leather tube for the vocal tract action. It produced different vowel sounds by manipulating the shape of the leather tube and consonant sounds were simulated by four separate constricted passages. Later in 1800s, Charles Wheatstone constructed his famous version of von Kempelen's speaking machine.

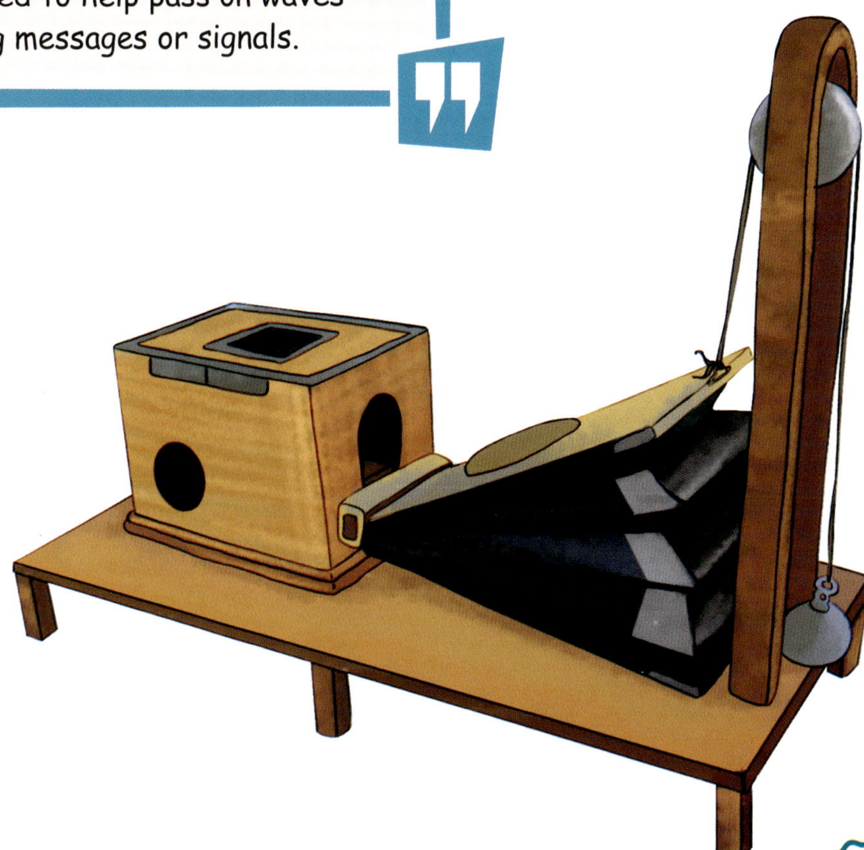

When was sound first recorded and played back on metal foil?

The phonograph was the first device that was used for recording and reproducing sound mechanically. It was invented by Thomas Edison in 1877. It had a thin sheet of tin foil wrapped around a hand-cranked, grooved, metal cylinder. It could play back sound by reading hollow cylinders that had the audio recording impressed on the outside surface. Later, wax was used as the recording medium for engraving instead of tin foil and came to be known as the Edison wax cylinder.

Find out

What is the full form of mp3?

Pocket fact

From Greek words!
The term 'phonograph' comes from two Greek words translated phonē and graphē meaning 'sound' and 'writing' respectively.

When was the digital audio player invented?

It was invented in 1979. The first portable digital audio player called the IXI was designed by British inventor Ken Kramer. It had a memory chip that could only store a few minutes of uncompressed audio. The high performance audio compression method later known as MP3 was developed between the late 1980s and early 1990s.

When was the first electric washing machine invented?

The first electric washing machine was introduced in 1908 by the Hurley Machine Company of Chicago, Illinois. It was invented by Alva J. Fisher and called the Thor. It resembled a drum with a galvanized tub and an electric motor. It had a series of blades that lifted the clothes as the cylinder rotated. After 8 rotations in one direction, the machine would reverse rotation so that the clothes did not wad up into a compact mass.

Find out

How much water does a dishwasher use in one cycle?

Pocket fact

No change!
Modern day washing machine was invented in 1908, and amazingly its design has not changed much in last 100 years.

When was the dishwasher invented?

The first practical dishwashing machine was invented in 1886 by Josephine Cochran. It was a hand operated machine with wire compartments to hold dishes which were sprayed with hot soapy water. It had a wheel that was turned using a hand crank on the outside the machine. This dishwasher was initially bought only by hotels and large restaurants. It was sold to the general public after the 1950s.

When was the first Smartphone invented?

The term smartphone was used by people in around 1995, but the first true smartphone was invented by IBM in 1992. It was called the Simon Personal Communicator. Apart from its calling features, the smartphone had a monochrome LCD touchscreen measuring 4.5 inches by 1.4 inches, and it came with a stylus. It could be used to send and receive emails, faxes, and pages.

Pocket fact

The toughest!
Sonim XP3300 Force is recognized as the toughest phone by Guinness World Records. It was dropped from 84ft and survived without any operational damage.

Find out

What is an e-book?

When was the first automated reader invented?

The world's first automated reader was invented by a school teacher Angela Ruiz Robles in Spain, 1949. She wanted to create a reader that would be far easier to carry for school children, than a number of different text books. This automated reader had a smaller amount of text printed onto spools and was operated by compressed air. This book was not electronic, yet it is hailed as the first automated reader.

When was the supercomputer invented?

The supercomputer was designed in 1964 by an electrical engineer Seymour Cray. Known as the CDC 6600, the supercomputer ran at a speed of 40 MHz and executed roughly three million floating-point operations per second. This made it the fastest computer in the world. Often considered to be the world's first supercomputer, the CDC 6600 was 10 times faster than most computers.

Pocket fact

So many jobs!
Supercomputers can do arithmetic jobs very fast. Hence they are used for code-breaking, weather forecasting, genetic analysis and other jobs that need many calculations.

Find out

Who built the internet?

When does the Internet face traffic?

The Internet is a global network connecting millions of computers worldwide. More than 190 countries are linked to one another and can share data and information. Internet traffic is the term used to describe the flow of data across the Internet. It happens when a lot of data is shared and received at the same time.

Index

A, B, C
alphabet
atmospheric
audio
bricks
bridges
brittle
chalk
chunks
clay-bearing
coarse
compartments
compressed
concrete
consonantal
corneal
cylinders

D, E, F
data
diameter
diaphragm
digital
drum
electrical
evolution
eyeglasses
flakes
foil

G, H
galvanized
gatherers
grains
graphite
gypsum
hand-carved
handwritten
harvest
hieroglyphs
holders
hunks
hunters
hydrogen

I, K
input
instrument
iron ore
kiln

L
leather
lens
lime

M, N
machine
mercury
microphone
modern
monochrome
mortar
notebook

P
parachute
phonograph
portable
pressure

S
smiths
socket
speech
spherical
spools
standard
steel
stylus
synthesizer

T, U, V, W
thermometer
tools
touch screen
tower
uncompressed
vocal
volcanic
wave
weapons
wrapping-paper